I am Josephine

(and I am a living thing)

To my parents, for first teaching me that I am an animal
and then telling me not to act like one. — J.T.

Many thanks to all my friends, new and old. — J.L.

Text © 2016 Jan Thornhill
Illustrations © 2016 Jacqui Lee

Owlkids Books acknowledges the financial support of the Canada Council for the Arts, the
Ontario Arts Council, the Government of Canada through the Canada Book Fund (CBF) and
the Government of Ontario through the Ontario Media Development Corporation's Book
Initiative for our publishing activities.

Published in Canada by
Owlkids Books Inc.
10 Lower Spadina Avenue
Toronto, ON M5V 2Z2

Published in the United States by
Owlkids Books Inc.
1700 Fourth Street
Berkeley, CA 94710

Library and Archives Canada Cataloguing in Publication

Thornhill, Jan, author
    I am Josephine : (and I am a living thing) / written by Jan Thornhill ;
illustrated by Jacqui Lee.

ISBN 978-1-77147-156-5 (bound)

    1. Mammals--Classification--Juvenile literature. 2. Animals--Classification--Juvenile
literature. 3. Mammals--Juvenile literature. 4. Life (Biology)--Juvenile literature. I. Lee, Jacqui,
illustrator II. Title.

QL706.2.T56 2016   j599   C2015-908009-6

Library of Congress Control Number: 2016930945

The artwork in this book was created in watercolor and assembled digitally.
Edited by: Karen Li
Designed by: Karen Powers

Manufactured in Dongguan, China, in May 2016, by Toppan Leefung Packaging & Printing
(Dongguan) Co., Ltd.
Job #BAYDC23

A   B   C   D   E   F

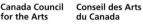

ONTARIO ARTS COUNCIL
CONSEIL DES ARTS DE L'ONTARIO
an Ontario government agency
un organisme du gouvernement de l'Ontario

Canada Council
for the Arts

Conseil des Arts
du Canada

Canadä

Publisher of Chirp, chickaDEE and OWL
www.owlkidsbooks.com

Owlkids Books is a division of

Bayard
CANADA

I am Josephine

(and I am a
living thing)

Written by
Jan Thornhill

Illustrations by
Jacqui Lee

OWLKIDS BOOKS

I am Josephine.

I am Josephine, and
I am a human being.

I am a **human being**, and so is my mom,
and so is my dad, and so is my baby brother, Felix.

BUS
STOP

CITY BUS

How many **human beings** can you find on this page?

I am Josephine,
and I am a mammal.

I am a **mammal**, and so is my mom,
and so is my dog, Cosmo, and so is a groundhog.

And so is that cat that's always
following me around. (Shoo, kitty!)

How many different kinds of mammals can you find on this page?

I am Josephine,
and I am an animal.

I am an **animal**, and so is my dad,
and so is a fish, and so is a deer, and so is
that mosquito that just bit me. (Ouch!)

How many different kinds of **animals**
can you find on this page?

I am Josephine,
and I am a living thing.

I am a **living thing**, and so is my brother, Felix, and so is a butterfly, and so is a tree, and so is a penguin.

How many different kinds of **living things** can you find on this page?

I am Josephine.
I am a human being.
I am a mammal.
I am an animal.
I am a living thing.

I am **all** of these things.

But I am still the only me—
Josephine!

Living things

* are made up of one or more tiny cells

* grow

* make copies of themselves (have babies)

* react to things around them

* need water and food (some make food from the Sun's energy)

* get rid of waste

* move in some way

Animals are living things that

* usually have a mother and a father (though many never know who their mothers and fathers are!)

* eat other living things

* digest food in a "stomach"

* can usually move around freely

Mammals are animals that

* usually have four legs
  (or two arms and two legs
  or flippers)

* give birth to live young (except
  for a few that lay eggs)

* feed their babies milk

* have hair or fur

* have warm blood

Human beings are mammals that

* stand upright

* walk on two legs

* can do many things with their
  hands and fingers

* have large busy brains

* talk to one another about
  a million different things

* remember what happened yesterday
  and imagine what might happen
  tomorrow

* make and use complicated tools

* make art and music for the
  pure joy of it

Josephine is a human being...and so are you.

Every human being is unique, which means there is no one else on Earth who is exactly like you!

What makes **you** different from other human beings?